Solo Book 2

Part of the definition of the word "extravaganza" is "an exciting show or event featuring extreme freedom of style and structure." Each solo in *Piano Extravaganza* features pianistic freedom within the style and form of the piece. Even when the hands move freely around the keyboard, my goal was to keep the technique required to play each piece within limited boundaries to ensure student success. I wanted the solos to feel comfortable in the hands, yet sound good and impressive to an audience. In addition, students playing the pieces should feel that they are creating interesting, yet worthwhile musical experiences, whether the piece is slow and introspective or fast and brilliant.

I hope that teachers, students, and audiences alike enjoy each musical extravaganza in this book.

Robert D. Vandall

Contents

Alfred Music
P.O. Box 10003
Van Nuys, CA 91410-0003
alfred.com

Copyright © 2014 by Alfred Music
All rights reserved

No part of this book shall be reproduced, arranged, adapted, recorded, publicly performed, stored in a retrieval system, or transmitted by any means without written permission from the publisher. In order to comply with copyright laws, please apply for such written permission and/or license by contacting the publisher at alfred.com/permissions.

ISBN-10: 1-4706-1453-7
ISBN-13: 978-1-4706-1453-9

Dennison Depot Blues

Robert D. Vandall

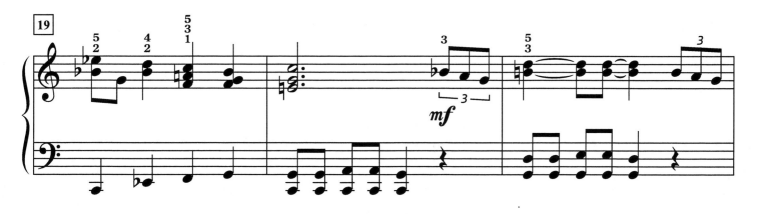

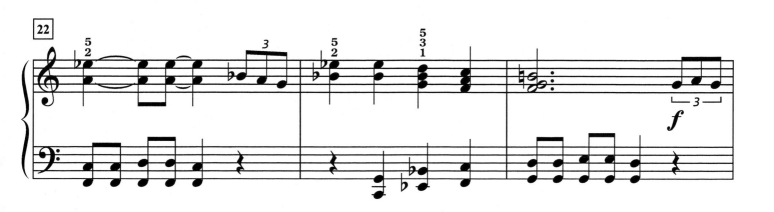

Grand Tarantella

Robert D. Vandall

Peaceful Moments

Robert D. Vandall

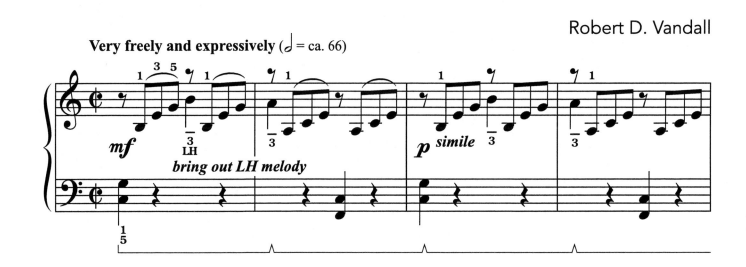

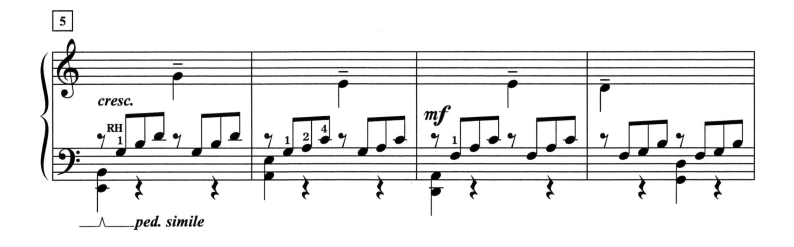

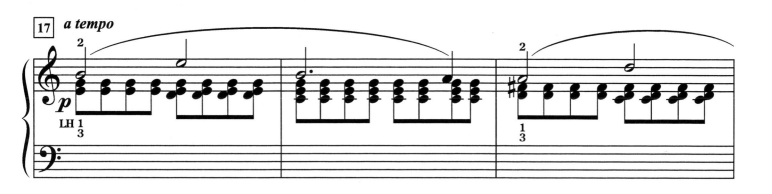

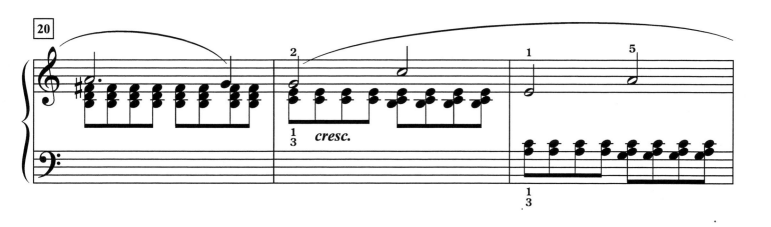

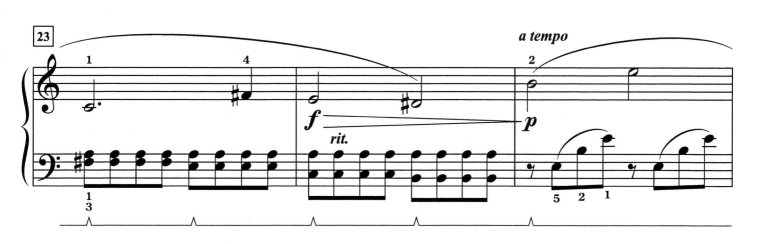

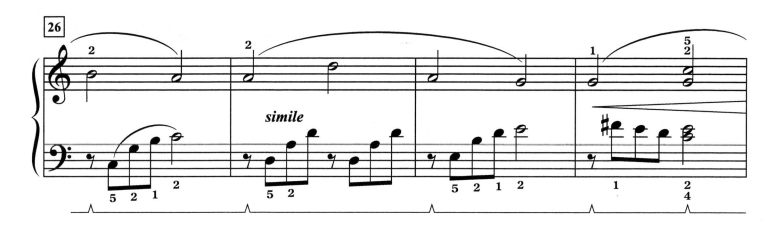

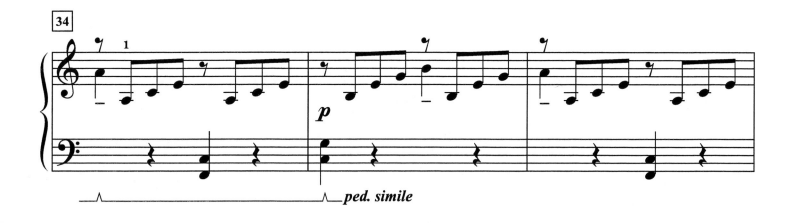

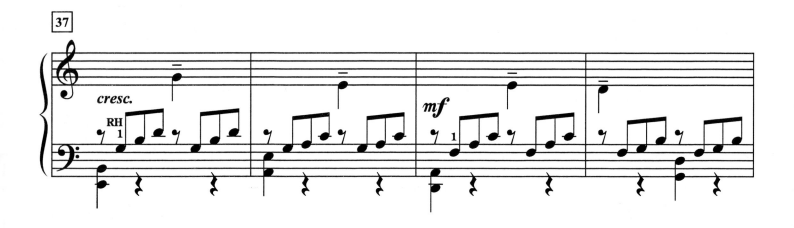

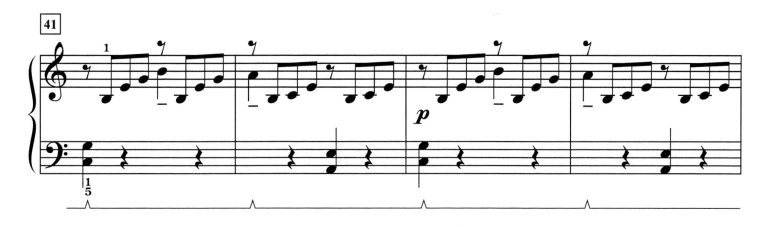

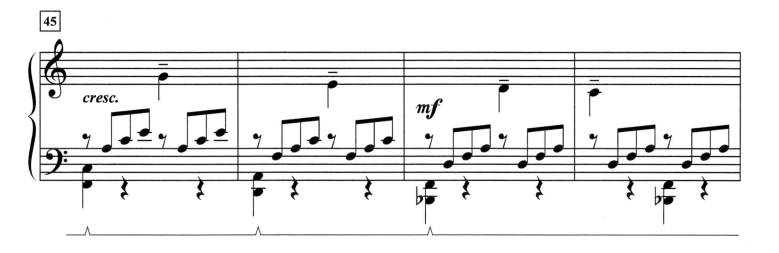

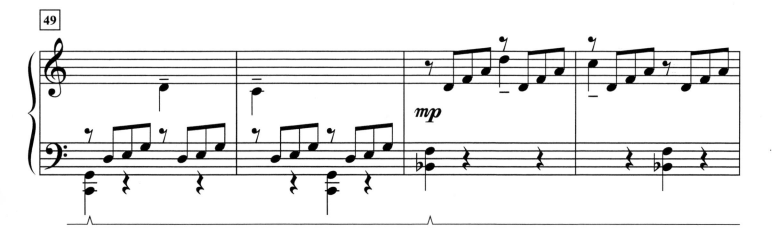

Holiday!

Robert D. Vandall

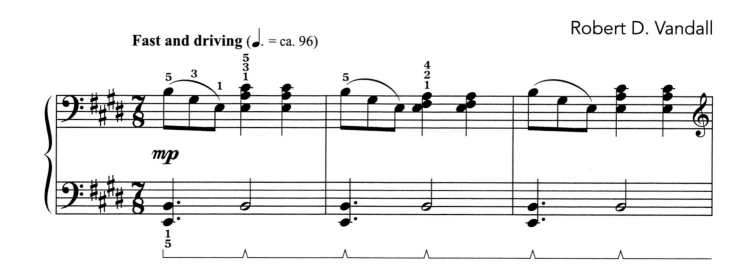

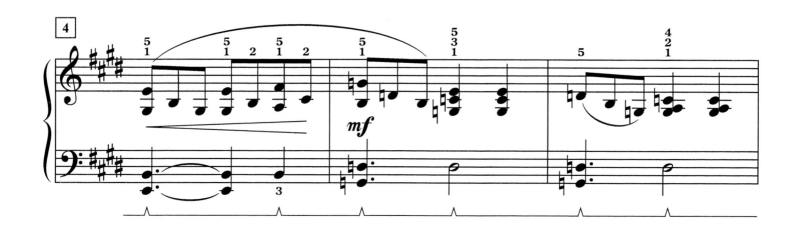

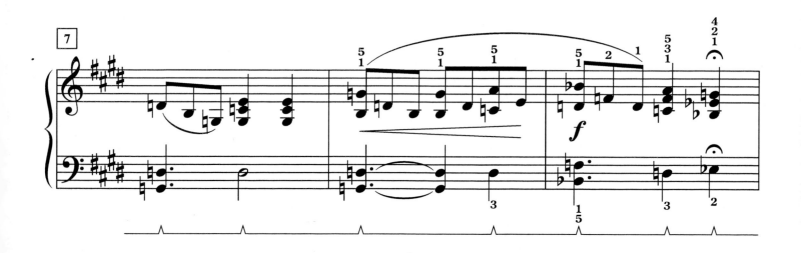

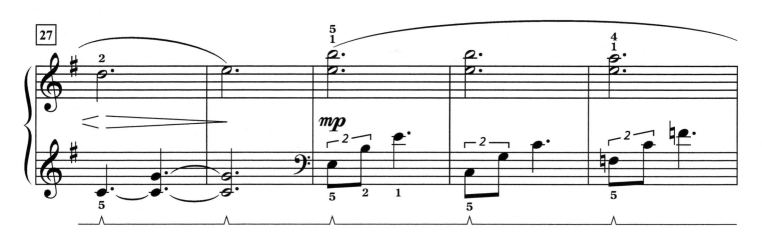

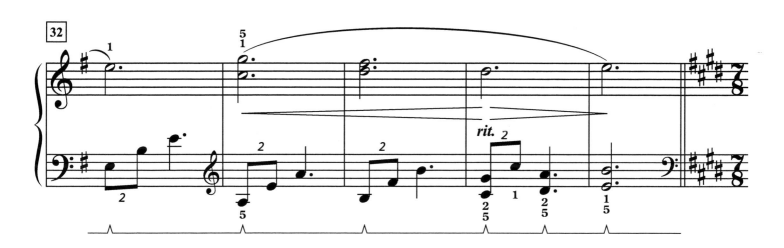

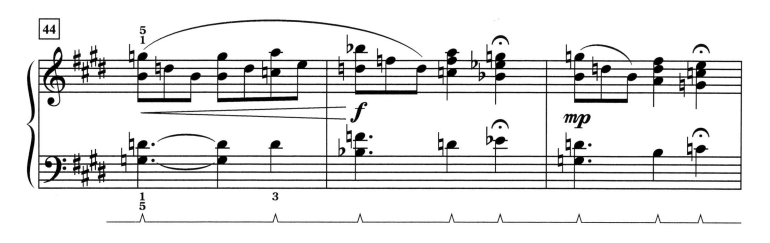

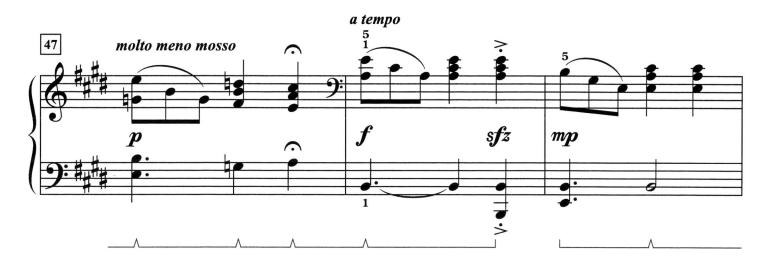

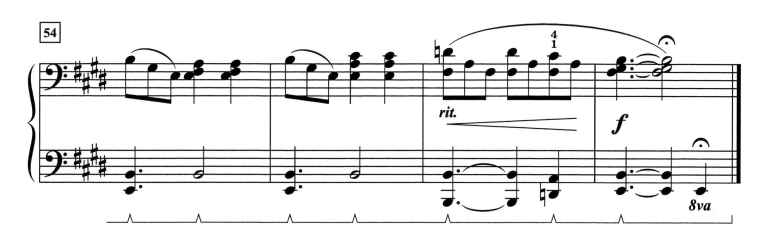

Stargazing Nocturne

Robert D. Vandall

Fairly quickly; much rubato ($\quarternote$ = ca. 120)

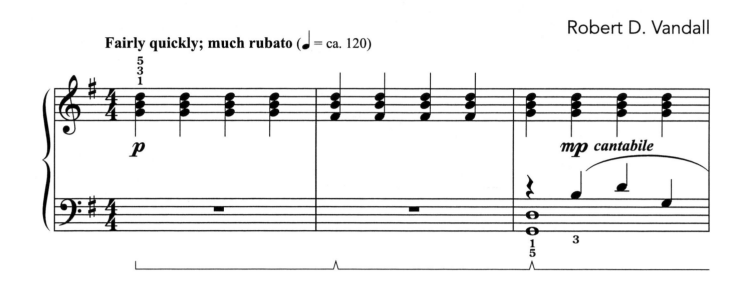

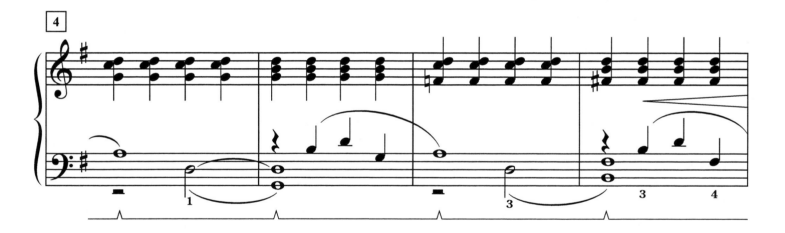

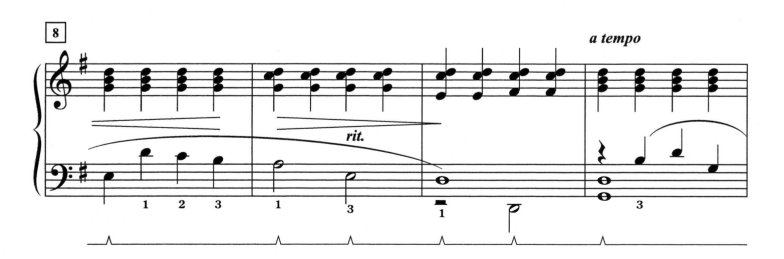

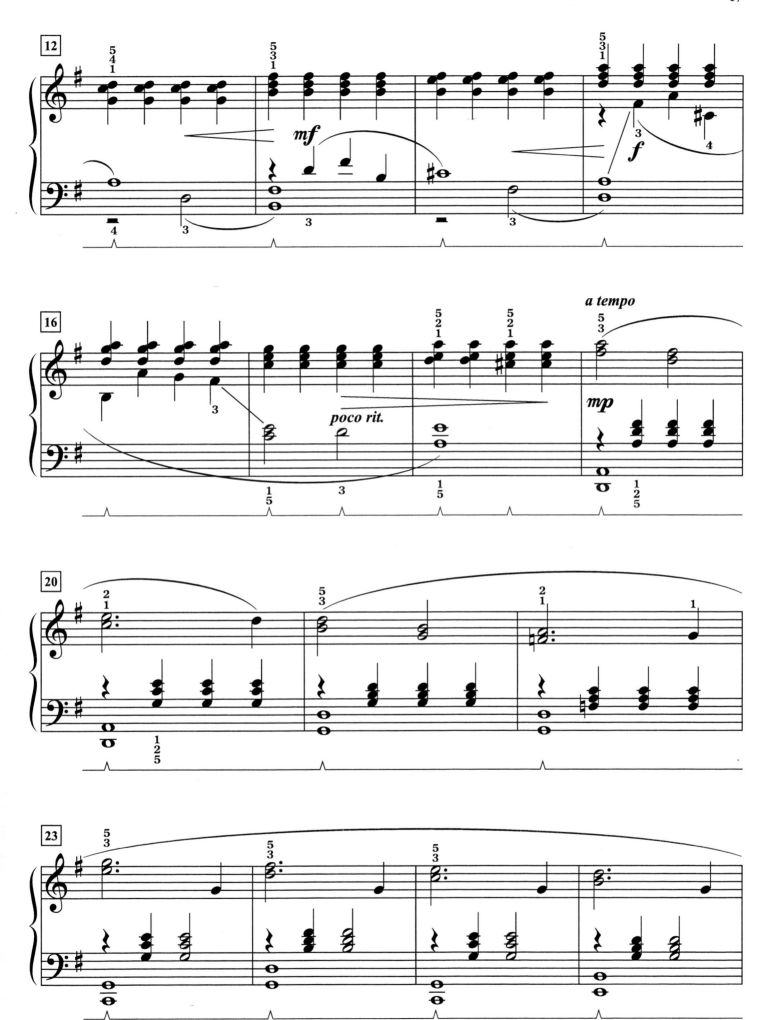

18

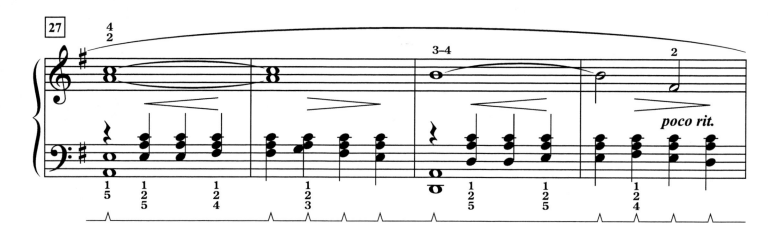

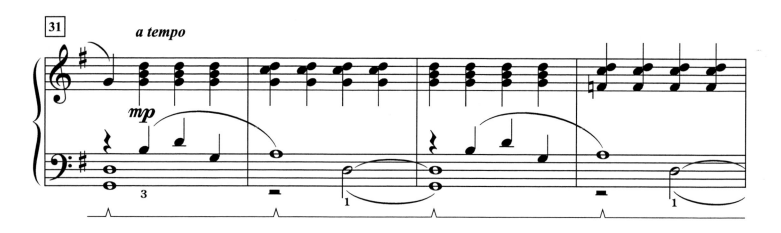

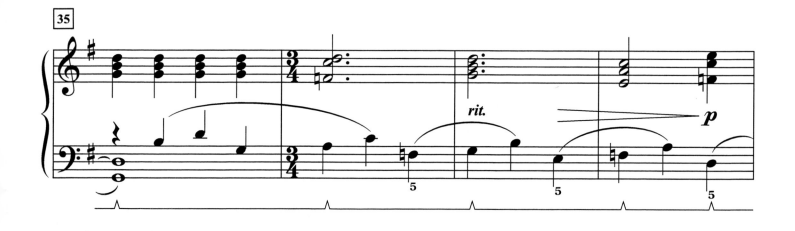

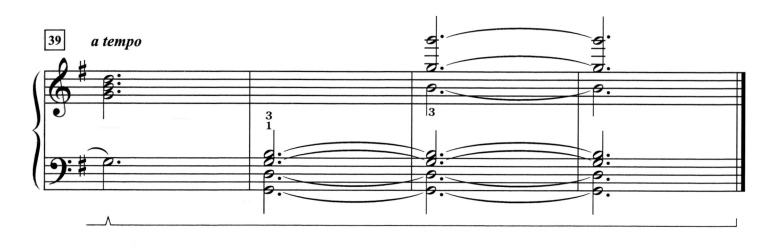

Fireworks

Robert D. Vandall

20

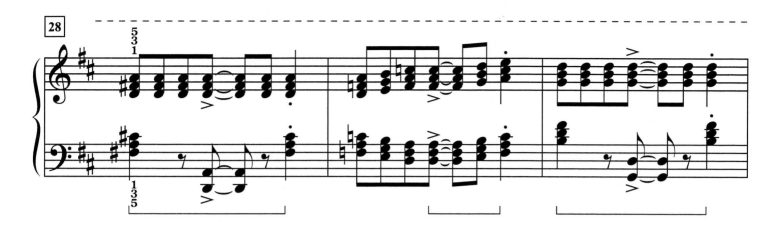

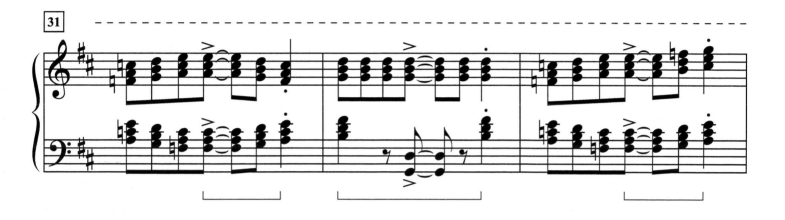

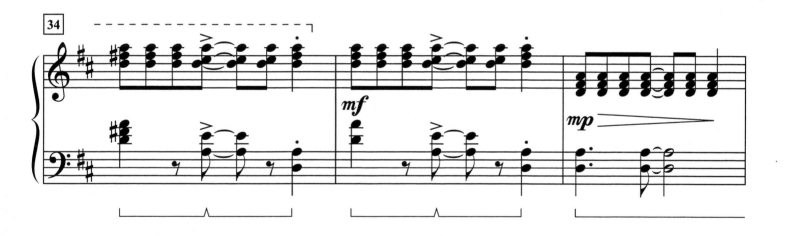

After the Storm

Robert D. Vandall

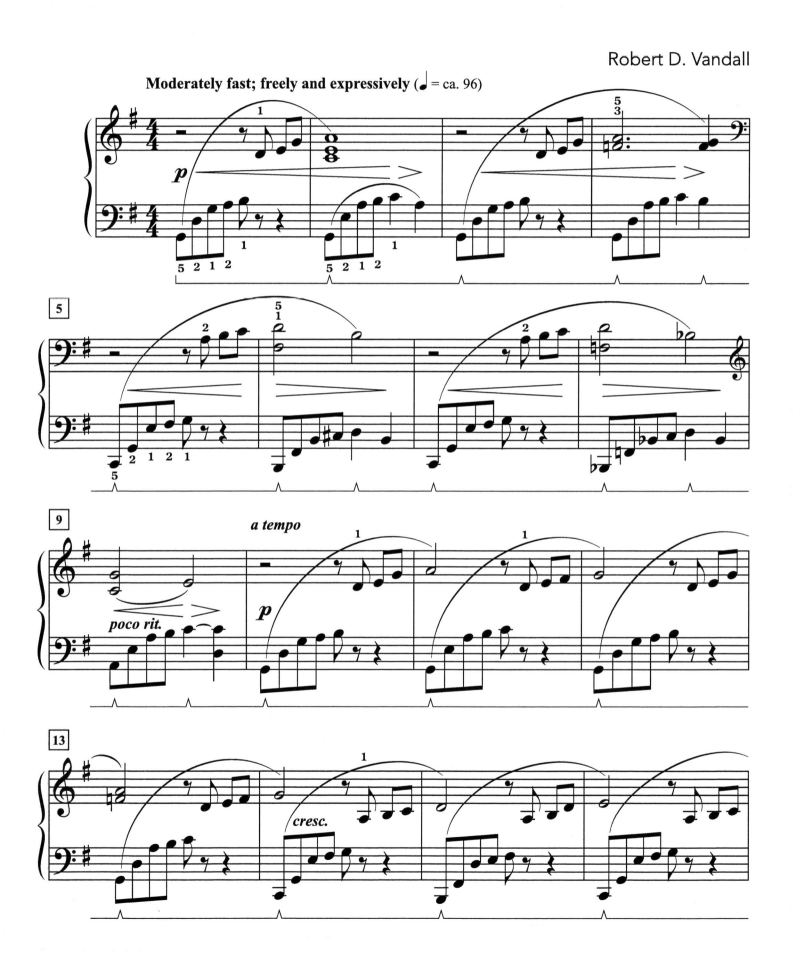